I0054205

Social Media Strategy for Everyone

By Amanda F. Potter

No part of this book may be reproduced or transmitted in any form or by any means, electronic or mechanical, including photocopying, recording, or by any information storage and retrieval system, without prior permission in writing from the author.

Copywrite: 2024 by Amanada Potter

Cover art design by: Katie Sterner, katiesterner.com

ISBN-13: 978-1-962699-27-3

Dedication

For Davey, who inspires me to "work hard and try not to mess up."

Chapter 1

It Starts with Strategy

Imagine this.

It's 2004. You're Mark Zuckerberg, a skinny nerd at Harvard, and you want an easy way to crowdsource ratings of the attractiveness of your classmates.

You have no idea you're about to change the world.

Potential hyperbole aside, 20+ years on from the advent of social media,[1] it isn't

---

[1] I say 20+ because it started well before Facebook, but Facebook arguably ushered in the explosion. What was the first social media platform? We could argue about that all day long, but why are you wasting time down here thinking about that?

optional anymore for any person, brand or company seeking to establish a digital presence. It's a must-have.

Too many people, though – even marketers! – think of it as an item to be checked off the list. "We have an Instagram account and Facebook account and are posting semi-regularly – check." They're often posting the same content across all platforms.

Or they may have started their account on a new, popular platform with high hopes that it would be the marketing equivalent of a silver bullet, but the novelty soon wore off – and so many other things required their attention – and pretty soon they felt good if they were just "getting something out there."

And then they can't figure out why their social media doesn't seem to be doing much for them.

Or they can't seem to figure out why their competitors' accounts are growing, while their accounts languish.

Or, if they've been lucky enough to hire or have access to a social media person or team, they can't seem to figure out why those people often seem burnt out and stressed. If they haven't had access to a social media person – if they're an artist, a writer, an entrepreneur, a small business owner, and they're trying to do it themselves – they too feel stressed out and overwhelmed. It's not getting them anywhere, and it's not fun anymore.

If any of that seems familiar to you, let me tell you that there is another way. You don't have to feel lost when it comes to your social media accounts.

The secret is starting with strategy.

*

There is a fallacy that is shared both by social media natives (Gen Z, I see you) and those of us who were introduced to social media later in life: that just being on social media is enough. It doesn't take any further thought beyond that!

When I interview candidates for entry-level social professional roles, I hear that kind of thinking all the time:

Me: "Tell me about how you stay on top of platform changes and best practices in social media."

Candidate: "Well, I'm just always on it, soooo…"

I hear it when I tell people what I do for work.

[BASED ON A TRUE STORY]

Me, at a barbecue: *sips drink*

Male acquaintance: "So, what do you do for work?"

Me: "Oh, I'm the content strategy manager for [insert name of company]."

Male acquaintance: *blinks*

Me: "I'm their social media manager."[2]

Male acquaintance: "Oh, I gotcha! Man, I'm surprised they have enough work for a full-time job for you."

Me, smiling through barely contained rage: *Enough work? I have a whole TEAM under me – and we can barely keep up!*

*

What separates the social media professional from the dilettante is the knowledge that there always needs to be a

---

[2]No, a social media manager and a content strategy manager are not the same thing, but sometimes that's the easiest way to explain it to people.

solid strategy behind your social media presence. I don't care if we're talking about the social media accounts for a large corporation, a small online retailer, or a solo artist or writer. What you do online needs to start with strategy; otherwise, you're always chasing the next shiny thing, or beating your head against the wall because you've been doing the same thing for some time and are seeing diminishing returns. Either way, it's not an effective use of your time, and it's not fun. And my philosophy? Let's make social media fun again.

This book is not for the seasoned social media professional. If that's you, odds are, you've got this down. Instead of reading this, turn off your notifications, go buy yourself a coffee and/or take a nap – you deserve it.

This book is for the person who wants to work on a social presence for themselves, their company, their nonprofit, etc., but just isn't sure where to start. Or maybe they've inherited some social accounts, and they know they could be better, but they're just not sure how to get there.

I'm here for you.

I've been in your place.

I'm not some social media wunderkind, or a digital native. I'm an elder millennial/young Gen X who didn't grow up with digital marketing. When I speak at colleges and high schools, the students often ask me if I studied social media in college. I have to laugh and tell them the internet barely existed when I was in college. Everything I've learned has been self-taught – both by following and reading some of the best content and social media strategy minds both past and present, but also by *doing the damn thing*. And not for sexy brands with huge budgets, either. For boring, nonsexy accounts, with zero budgets, as the only social media staff.

Brands with a small team but no real understanding of what in the world they are doing on social media.

Brands that made me wonder, "What in the world are we going to talk about on Facebook today?"

Brands that made me think, "Why in the world would anyone follow us?" Brands that made me think, "How am I going to pull this thing off, and with zero budget, and a creative team whose priorities are in a million other directions?"

Brands that are unconvinced, even skeptical, about the benefit of investing in social to their bottom line.

But you know what? That was the best way to start my career in social media. The stakes were low – no one cared about my rinky-dink Facebook page – and leadership didn't really have me or my work on their radar (until I messed up or there was a crisis, that is!). And I had to learn the hard way how to hustle for an audience, how to figure out content that worked, and how to live symbiotically with the cruel mistress we call platform algorithms. (More on this one later.)

I didn't have an audience. I built one. And I learned some lessons – and formed some personal philosophies and best practices along the way. That's what I'm here to share with you. My secrets really aren't that secret – but they don't seem to be common knowledge, either. But as the kids say, I'm not here to gatekeep. I'm here to help. Consider me your social media mentor.

Let's get started.

Chapter 2

That Time a Big Green Bird Dominated TikTok

Now let me fast forward you over a dozen years. You're not Mark Zuckerberg anymore. It's now 2021, and you're Zaria Parvez, the newly appointed head of social at Duolingo, a language learning platform and app. You set your sights on TikTok, a social media platform that blew up during the pandemic and is making a whole lot of noise, especially with Gen Z.

Previously, Duolingo's brand strategy on TikTok made sense. It focused on videos about the nuances of different languages, interesting language facts, language history, etc. Totally in line with a brand that sells language learning

9

services, right? And their following was decent enough.

But you decide to blow that shit up.

You know that TikTok is different. The younger demographic on the platform wants inside jokes, memes, and ridiculousness. They want things that seem a bit – well, a bit unhinged, to be honest.

And you decide to give the people what they want.

The star of your account is now a life-sized costume of your mascot, a giant green cartoon bird. You start a running joke about your obsession with the singer Dua Lipa. You jump on trending audio and, perhaps more importantly, trending jokes. You understand that the shelf life of these jokes is incredibly short on this platform – they could be irrelevant in a day or two, so you know you need to move fast before the legal team can even start to evaluate. In fact, working outside of the legal team becomes one of your running jokes. Your videos seem low-budget but clever, tongue-in-cheek, and – perhaps most importantly – they show a real understanding of the platform and what's happening on it.

And your strategy *works*.

Under the guidance of Parvez, Duolingo's TikTok account has grown from 50,000 followers to over 12 million, with an engaged audience that actively waits for and interacts with their videos.

And while the platform growth is exciting, what brands should really pay attention to is the community that Duolingo has built. Who among us wouldn't want an engaged consumer base who is not just tolerating what we put online, but *excited* about it? Who among us doesn't covet not just the likes – which are arguably cheap – but the comments, saves and shares that propel organic growth and cause the algorithm to serve the videos to more and more people?

I can hear the C-suite-ish among us asking: *"But was there a return on investment?"* You bet there was. As a result of their focus on social media marketing and community building, Duolingo has these numbers to show for themselves.

	2021	2023
Monthly Active Users (MOUs)	37 million	74 million
Daily Active Users (DAUs)	9.1 million	21.4 million
Revenue	$250 million	$21.4 million

"Duolingo Revenue and Usage Statistics." The Business of Apps

Now, it would be easy for people to take the wrong lesson from this case study. They might look at Duolingo's TikTok account and think either:

a) My brand needs to be doing exactly that. I don't know how or why, but just…that.

and/or

b) Their account is just having fun. It has no real strategy behind it.

Au contraire, mon cherie.

The reason why Duolingo's videos on TikTok took off is because they made sense for the platform and for the audience they were trying to reach. They hired someone with a deep understanding of the platform, who wasn't afraid to go all in on TikTok culture. They made it make sense for their brand.

Would something like that make sense for your brand? Maybe. I can't tell you that. Only you can – and hopefully, only after some serious reflection on your goals, target audiences, and staffing capabilities – which we are about to get into.

Chapter 3

I Wasn't Lying about the Whole Strategy Thing, Guys

If you are feeling guilty because up to this point, you thought social just kind of *happened*, and you never really gave thought to the whys or hows or shoulds, don't fret. I have seen many a seasoned marketer throw all their marketing knowledge out the window when it comes to social. Somehow, a lot of us seem to have blinders on to the kind of strategy we need to employ when we're thinking about this unique digital space. I think it's because social media strategy is invisible to the casual observer, and good social media strategy can look easy and low effort.

Much like PR and political strategy, it can take months of planning to look spontaneous. I watched with interest when U.S. Representative Katie Porter just *happened* to get photographed reading Mark Manson's *The Subtle Art of Not Giving a F*ck* on the United States House of Representatives floor during the Kevin McCarthy confirmation hearings for Speaker of the House. The photo went viral. Within a week, I got a fundraising email for Porter's Senate campaign. I hadn't signed up for her email list – but her campaign knew that I fit within a certain demographic that had probably seen and was entertained by the viral photo.

Politics aside, my point is that the best social strategy is exactly like that. It seems spontaneous but is actually built on a deep understanding of your target audience – all the while not necessarily screaming THIS IS MARKETING! THIS IS THE MESSAGE I WANT YOU TO GET!

Sound hard? Yeah, man. It's hard as shit. But it's also a fun challenge for the right kind of masochist.

Now, good social media strategy doesn't always look effortless. Sometimes, as with big ad campaigns, you can see how much time, energy and money went into it. There is a lot to be said for polished creative. The cases for polished versus off-the-cuff content will come later.

*

The other reason why I talk so much about the importance of social media strategy is because we still need a shift in how it is categorized as a career discipline. Even after all these years, people still see the job of social media as an executional one – pressing "send" on content and getting it onto a platform. Anyone who has worked on social for longer than five minutes understands that it's so much more than that. I learned the hard way that the only way you can change this mindset is to develop and then talk about social media strategy that's rooted in specific, measurable goals.

*

Oh, how I wish those jokes about the intern running a major brand's social accounts would just die, already.

You know the ones I'm talking about. Some company puts out a cringey, error-ridden, tone-deaf, or just plain poorly timed piece of content, and all of a sudden the rest of the internet starts in with the same old jokes and comments: "Someone's going to get fired." "Looks like it's that intern's last day."

Setting aside the fact that it's hard to do your job perfectly 100% of the time, even when your job is publishing content on incredibly public (and merciless) online platforms.

Setting aside the fact that everyone makes mistakes in their jobs, but they don't usually get dunked on by the general public.

Setting all of that aside, savvy organizations and people who work in social both know the same thing: *running social accounts for an organization is not a job for an intern.*

A company's online presence – up to and including social media – is incredibly important. It drives sentiment, creates (or destroys) community, and provides a real-time connection to your audience. It's not just marketing; it's PR, crisis communications, branding, market research, and development.

Controlling and coordinating all of that is the job of a circus ringmaster or a symphony conductor, depending on the day.

A lot of brands get it – to some extent. Social and content professionals are getting more and more respect, more and more responsibility, and increasingly high-level titles. Yet, there's still a frustrating number of people who think social media is no more than pressing a "send" button – especially if the social media professional has creative professionals helping him or her create content. Many leaders still see the social role as an operational one, rather than a strategic one. That's shortsighted, and a recipe for a) ineffective content and b) frustrated staff.

Like the title of this book says, social media is inherently a strategic endeavor that takes thought, research, and planning. As a whole, it's not off-the-cuff – although it can and should be timely and responsive to online trends – or unplanned. It's not an intern twiddling their thumbs and trying to come up with something, *anything*, to say. It's also not the place where you replicate your other marketing channels, dumping commercials and other hard-selling content without a second thought.

For a long time, social media accounts for businesses and organizations were seen as transactional. Posts were to be vehicles to get people somewhere else – usually a website – to sell things. The formula was a basic sales copy model: copy and graphics touting your product (whether that's goods, services, or ideas) ending with a call to action to lead the user somewhere else.

That time, too, needs to be over. Social media is now old enough to drink, and it's nothing new for brands to have a presence on it. People are savvier than ever, and they're tired. Time for a hard truth: no one is going on their favorite social media platform to see your commercial or hear your sales pitch. They're going online to be educated, entertained, or informed. And if you're not doing that, you're wasting your time. People will scroll on by. You're also adding to the noise – with so many users and brands on social platforms, it gets harder and harder for content even to get seen.

If you aren't giving people something of value, you don't stand a chance. That takes thought.

That takes – say it with me now – strategy.

*

But I'm preaching to the choir. You've picked up this book because you know social media is important and you want to be better at it. Or maybe you've just been told that social media is important, but you're not sure why.

Maintaining a presence across social media is all about brand identity. Brand identity is all about winning two battles: getting people to a) *know* who you are and b) *like* who you are. In other words, brand awareness and brand affinity. And when you have a solid, easily identifiable brand identity, it increases the perceived value of whatever you're selling. It increases your legitimacy and professionalism.

However, I've seen many cases when having a rock-solid brand can go too far, especially online. Suddenly, it's less about content that makes sense for your audience and the platforms you're on, and more about adhering to your brand's look and identity. (If you're nodding your head and thinking "Yes, that's how it should be," consider this a virtual face slap and then read on to learn why NO, that is *not* how it should be.) Having a solid social media strategy will keep you from becoming a slave to your brand identity. It gives you a guide rather than a prescription.

Chapter 4

You Have to Walk Before You Run, and Other Annoying Aphorisms Exemplified

First things first: understanding social media as a whole.

"Wait a minute, Amanda," I can hear you thinking. "I thought the whole premise of this book was that strategy comes first."

Yes, you are right. But there are a few things I want to make sure you understand about social media before we jump into the first thing so that you can create the best strategy possible. So. Here are the first things before the first thing.

1. Social media platforms run on algorithms, as a rule. There may be one out there that doesn't, but I can't think of it.

If you're rolling your eyes and saying, "DUH Amanda, everyone knows that" – then great, skip ahead.

If you don't know what the heck I'm talking about – buckle up.

There's a reason why you see what you see on social media. Every platform is using a sophisticated math equation to try to serve you the kind of content it thinks you want to see.

Depending on the algorithm (i.e. math equation), it is weighing your likes, comments, shares, saves, time spent watching videos, replays of videos, etc. It may measure how quickly you scroll by certain content versus if you pause slightly longer on other content. It is measuring this down to the second – or millisecond.

Why?

That gets us to the next thing.

2. Social media platforms are there to make money for the companies that own them.

Read that again.

They are not there for the greater good.

They are not there to help you make money.

They are not there to make you feel good about yourself.

They are not there to make the world a better place.

They are there to make someone money. And it's not you.

Now, I get it. You are reading this book because, presumably, you are interested in harnessing social media to help yourself make money. That's great! We can do that. But you need to understand that the primary goal of various platforms is notX to help you do that, per se. Sure, they want your advertising dollars. But in the end, their goal is to make themselves money. Not you.

I've seen "personalized" marketing advice from "account executives" at the world's largest social media platform (as of 2024) that was shared with various businesses. The marketing advice was all the same. It wasn't personalized for business needs. It was geared to get businesses to spend more money and make the platform profit more.

Make no mistake. These social media platforms are not watching out for you. As of this writing, the largest ones have slashed their customer support, even for accounts that spend seven figures in ads annually (like the ones I work on in my day job). That's why you must be savvy and watch out for yourself.

3. Social media algorithms are constantly evolving – and they aren't transparent about those updates. Furthermore, each platform will have a different algorithm – even platforms that are owned by the same company (like Meta, which owns both Facebook and Instagram). That's one reason why the idea of taking one piece of content and posting it across all your social accounts is not a good one – different algorithms are going to prioritize different kinds of content (not to mention the difference between your audiences on said platforms).

The best practice would be to read social media industry websites, newsletters, emails, blogs, etc. – the same as any other industry.

But even better – see what works for you. Test and retest. The algorithm is one thing, but the way YOUR audience reacts to YOUR content is going to be something else entirely.

4. Nothing is free, and you don't own your presence on a social media platform. Going back to number 2 – social media platforms are using your content, activity, and information to a) sell ads and b) sell information to advertisers. Hey, that works great for you, since you may well want to advertise on social media at some point! But it's also good to remember that everything you post on a social platform usually becomes the property of the platform to use as they wish. If you want more details about what they will be doing with it, read your user agreement in detail. Also, remember that you are at the whims of the platform. If it disappears tomorrow, so does your content. If the algorithm changes in a way that doesn't prioritize your content – sorry, Charlie. Go back to your strategy and evolve.

That's the modern Catch-22 – you need to be on social to reach your audience, but you don't own your platform. Like it or leave it –

literally. Frustrating? Yep. But that's the name of the game.

Okay. Those four points may have seemed a little depressing, and I apologize for that. But I want you to come into this with clear eyes and a realistic sense of what you're up against when you're planning your social media strategy – and an understanding of why it's important to invest in a *strategy* rather than just a *presence*. A presence is subject to the whims of an algorithm and gets stymied real quick. A strategy is a living thing, able to evolve with your needs and the changing digital landscape.

And that's an exciting thing!

So, are you still with me? Onward!

Chapter 5

Know Your People. No, Not Those People. The People You Want to Know. (Your Audience!)

Whether you're thinking about your social media strategy for a particular campaign or for your brand as a whole, the steps are the same. And once you have them down, they'll become second nature – and your social media efforts will be so much more effective. You'll have a "true north" to guide your efforts, so you don't waste time and energy chasing tactics that yield no results.

I like to think about the process in four steps.

Step One: Know your audience, and what you want from them.

Identifying your audience is one of the basic tenets of marketing, but I see it happen over and over: the words "social media" enter the chat, and all of a sudden there's this feeling that you need to be all things to all people.

You know what that is? That's a recipe for playing it safe and being boring.

And being boring is the cardinal sin of social media.

How do you know if your content is boring your audience? Nothing's happening. You have low reach. Your accounts aren't growing. Your content isn't being saved or shared. You're not hitting your key metrics – whether it's reach, clicks, or engagement.

At the same time, it's a common mistake to be super unclear or squishy about what you want your audience to do as a result of your social media post. That's another recipe for failure. You have to know what action you want your audience to take to know if your post is successful. Maybe you don't want them to buy something or click on a link. Maybe all you want is for your audience to feel *good* about your brand. Okay, that's a thing. An important thing, in fact. Now that you know what you want from people, it can guide what you create – compelling visuals and/or copy that will grab people, hold their attention, and make them associate your brand with X emotion.

Speaking of metrics – we can't talk about audience and avoid talking about metrics. You can't spray and pray, and you can't be moving so fast that you don't have time to take a look at how your content is performing. Your analytics are everything. They tell you so much: what and how your audience thinks of your content, and by extension, YOU. But what metrics should you be paying attention to?

It depends.

Manu Muraro, who runs Your Social Team and Your Template Club, says the metrics you need to track are the ones that align with your goals. In other words, there's no one-size-fits-all metric – not in social media in general, and not for your brand or company.

If you want to...	You need to measure...
Build brand recognition/ awareness	Reach, likes, comments, retweets, shares
Grow followers	Shares
Add value	Saves, shares
Get conversions (email sign ups, sales, etc.)	Link clicks, profile visits

If you don't know exactly what those terms above mean, no worries! I've got you. Here are some of the most common social media metrics and their basic definitions. There are nuances depending on the platform, of course, but I'll try to simplify them by the most common denominator here.

Reach: the total number of unique users who have seen your content

You can visualize your reach number as actual people. Your reach is 4,765? Your piece of content has been in front of 4,765 individual people. If that's still hard to think about, think of 4,765 bobbleheads. Or 4,765 different cats, all with unique names and personalities. Whatever you need to do. I'm not here to judge you. Anyway, that one is easy enough, right?

Impressions: the total number of times your content is displayed, regardless of whether it has already been served to that person or not

So, it's useful to look at impressions and reach together, when possible, because you can evaluate your frequency and relevancy. If both reach and impressions are high, you can deduce that your content may be resonating with your audience, and your message is spreading effectively. However, some platforms don't offer both reach and impression numbers.

Your impressions should be higher than reach because your content could be shown multiple times to the same person. That's the frequency number I mentioned in the paragraph above.

When you get into paid placements, some platforms such as Facebook have controls to limit the times your ad is shown to a person. We've all been there. We keep seeing the same annoying social media ad over and over. We don't want to be that advertiser.

Engagement Rate: the percentage of people who interacted with your content out of the total number of people who saw it (likes, comments, shares)

Engagement rate is one of the most crucial metrics. It tells you whether your audience is interested in your content. (It does not, however, tell you if your audience likes your content, but you will usually see that reflected in the comments and reactions!)

The different kinds of engagements will do different things for you, especially on different platforms. Comments and reactions are good general engagement to help you see how people feel about your content and to help your content continue to rank in the algorithm. Shares are typically very valuable because that leads to your content being seen by people who aren't following your account. Shares are what lead to things going viral. Saves are also a valuable engagement action, and something both the almighty algorithm and you should like seeing – it means your audience found your content valuable enough to want to bookmark it to come back to it later.

The one area where you must tread carefully with engagement rate is on ads and boosted posts. You can optimize for engagement, which sounds great. And it can be! But then just know that Facebook – or whatever platform you're using – is actively choosing users who are most likely to engage with content, so at that point, it does not tell you if your content is good or not. It just tells you that you bought engagement – which again, is useful, but shouldn't be confused with organic interest. If you want to know if your audience loves your content, look at organic engagement – or look at the engagement on ads optimized for reach or clicks.

Average engagement rate: a metric used for platform, industry, and brand benchmarking.

People will often ask what the average engagement rate for a given platform is so they can measure their performance against it. That's a great question. It changes all the time, so I would suggest searching the internet for the latest information[3]. Simply search "Average engagement rate for [platform] [year]."

You will want to know how to calculate engagement rate so you also set your own benchmarks. It's pretty easy once you get used to it.

The equation for your engagement rate is the number **of engagements divided by impressions or reach.**

---

[3] You can also easily find this information online for other common social media metrics, like click-through rates, engagement, etc. The information you get is going to vary, so look at a few sources and try to get an idea of a range. Some reputable sources are Hootsuite, Sprout Social, Emplifi, Rival IQ, DataReportal and Statista.

$$\text{Engagement Rate} - \left(\frac{\text{Likes} + \text{Comments} + \text{Shares}}{\text{Total Impressions or Reach}} \right) \times 100$$

Should you use impressions or reach as your dividing number? It's most common to use impressions. I like to use reach because I want to know out of the individual people who saw my content, how many took some kind of action. However, most industry numbers divide by impressions, so I have to know that my engagement numbers will then look high compared to industry or platform benchmarks. I'm cooking the books a bit, which is an important caveat when you're trying to tell an honest story about performance to your stakeholders!

The tl;dr[4] here? If you aren't sure if you should calculate your engagement rate by impressions or reach, just use impressions – especially if you want to benchmark against platform or industry standards.

---

[4] too long; didn't read

Click–Through Rate (CTR): the percentage of people who clicked on a link in your post relative to the number who saw it

This is a valuable metric if you have a post that leads people elsewhere – like to your website. If your CTR is low, you may want to evaluate if you've given your audience enough of a reason to click – or if you've even caught their attention at all.

The equation for CTR is the number of clicks divided by impressions.

$$CTR = \left(\frac{\text{Total Clicks}}{\text{Total Impressions}} \right) \times 100$$

Conversion Rate: the percentage of users who completed a desired action (like purchasing or signing up) after clicking on your social media content

As with CTR and engagement rate, the formula for this is straightforward: the number of conversions divided by impressions. However, to measure conversions, you generally need to either use a third-party tool such as Google Analytics or implement something like a Facebook pixel (Google it!) onto your website. These tools will help you track user traffic from your social media content to your website to calculate conversions.

Follower Growth Rate: the rate at which your social media following is growing over a specific period

This is pretty easy to understand, right? An easy way to measure this is simply to subtract the difference between your current following and the previous period's follower number (whether it's last month, last year, or whatever), and then divide that number by the previous time period's follower count. Multiply that by 100, and you have your percentage growth.

$$\text{Follower Growth Rate}(\%) = \left(\frac{\text{New Followers} - \text{Old Followers}}{\text{Old Followers}} \right) \times 100$$

Here's an example with actual numbers. Let's say that you start the month with 5,000 followers, and you end it with 5,500.

$$\text{Follower Growth Rate(\%)} - \left(\frac{5,500 - 5,000}{5,000}\right) \times 100 - \left(\frac{500}{5,000}\right) \times 100 - 10\%$$

Your follower growth rate was 10%. In one month! Great work!

Still confused? That's okay. Just Google "percent increase calculator" and you'll get a number of sites that will do the math for you.

Share of Voice (SOV): measures the percentage of all online content and conversations about your industry or topic that are generated by your brand and/or conversations about your brand (depending on how you have your measurements set up).

The definition above was a mouthful, so I like to tell people to think of SOV like this. You're at a party with 100 people. Of those 100 people, 53 are talking about your brand. 47 are talking about your competitor. That would give your brand a 53% share of voice and your competitor a 47% share of voice.

SOV is one of my favorite measurements to help people understand the power of online content. It's not something that you can easily measure on your own, but certain social media tools such as Hootsuite have built-in tools for measuring SOV – including color-coded data visualizations to share with stakeholders.

Sentiment: evaluates the emotional tone of user comments and mentions about your brand, determining whether they are positive, negative, or neutral

This is a useful metric when you want to see the overall tone of chatter about your brand online. As with share of voice, sentiment is something that is easiest to measure with the use of a tool.

You will want to look at your analytics campaign by campaign – if not post by post. At the same time, don't get too freaked out by the month-to-month change in numbers. It's often more useful to look at how things like audience growth are looking on a quarterly basis.

Chapter 6

Go Where Your People Are (and Be the Wallflower Taking Notes)

You've figured out who your target audience is. You know what your goals are and what metrics you want to measure. Now you need to do some research and figure out what your target audience's favorite social media platforms are.

Step Two: Figure out what platforms your audience is on – and how they are using those platforms.

Whether that's through formal or informal market research, or by just googling the demographics of the top social media platforms, you need to find out what virtual sandbox your audience is playing in – so you can join them there!

Creating an account or maintaining a presence on a certain social platform because it's big, or it's trendy, or it's easy for you, is not a solid strategy. Going back to the playground analogy, if everyone's in the sandbox, you can't stand 100 yards away by the slide and expect everyone to join you there. They're having a great time where they're at! It would take a compelling case to get people to follow you to a platform they're not otherwise on. Maybe a world-class brand with a hefty marketing budget could do it. *Maybe*. But to me, that sounds like an exercise in frustration for most brands. Why waste your resources? Why not go where your people are?

The next mistake a lot of brands make is thinking that just being present on their ideal platform is enough. Hate to break it to you, but it's not. You need to make sure your content

makes sense for the nuances of the platform –
which is exactly what Duolingo did in the case
study at the start of this section.

More bad news – this may require digging
beneath the surface a bit. It requires spending
some time on the platform, to get to know the
culture there. Again, look at the Duolingo
example. Their early content made sense for
TikTok – on the surface. It was video content
about learning languages featuring young,
attractive people. So why didn't it go viral until
they switched their strategy?

It's because at first, they missed the ethos
of early TikTok: the culture of unhinged
zaniness, inside jokes, the trending audio and
jokes, the shying away from hard sells. And it
wasn't until they hired a pro who understood
TikTok and started creating TikTok-specific
content that they really seemed to take off. At
the same time, their presence on the platform
suddenly seemed to make sense. It started to
feel *organic,* which was and is crucial to that
time and space. It seemed like they were
having fun rather than trying to get you to buy
something from them, which also was crucial to

the platform. By doing all that, they were able to connect with their audience on a new level.

If you're reading this and thinking, "So does that mean I shouldn't be using the same piece of content across all my social media platforms?" Then bravo! You are exactly where you need to be. Social media marketing publishing tools like to use the ability to place one piece of content on multiple social media sites as a selling feature. Hot take: *it's not.* Sure, it's helpful. I use that capability all the time. But I also know that I have to be careful to differentiate my content – even in small ways – to fit the platform I'm sending it to.

That last part is crucial. Yes, you should change your content to fit the platform. No, it doesn't have to be completely different content. It doesn't even have to be massive changes. This is how we did it at a sports network I worked for.

Every week during high school basketball season, the sports network would name athletes of the week for high school boys and girls basketball. The producer working on the segment would create a video to go with the announcement. This is how athlete of the week was placed on different platforms, and why:

Facebook: We knew Facebook was where the parents, grandmas, grandpas, coaches, and school accounts were. We knew that all of those people would want to share like crazy. So, we were careful to make sure that we posted the boys and girls winners in separate posts, with the video showing their highlights. We tagged any school or team accounts we could find, which was a lot of extra work – but it paid off. The posts got shared like crazy and were consistently high-performing posts every week.

Twitter/X: We used much of the same creative as we did on Facebook, but we also experimented with the size of the graphic. We found that using a slightly longer graphic – think the size of a baseball card, rather than a square or horizontal orientation – worked better. It took up more space when people were scrolling on phones, so our theory was that people tended to slow down and pay more attention to those tweets. Of course, we also tagged the teams, schools, and athletes, so they would retweet. Again, finding those handles took a lot of time – you've never struggled until you've tried to find and verify the Twitter handles for random small-town high school basketball teams – but adding them always paid off.

Instagram: We considered the Instagram Feed and the Instagram Story to be two different placements due to the different consumer behaviors.

On the feed, we shared a carousel with both the girls winner and the boys winner included in the same post. We did this because at that time, Instagram was prioritizing carousel content, making it show up more often in people's feeds. Of course, we tagged the athletes and teams in the content, making it easy for them to share – and another benefit of the carousel was that it gave the athletes and teams an option of which creative they wanted to share on their stories.

For our Instagram Story placements, we didn't just share our post to the story. We created graphics specifically for that vertical size placement and also tagged the athletes and teams there so they could share it on their stories. We wanted to make sure it was something they'd be proud to share on their own stories, so we made the Story placements a little more cool and edgy than our usual brand look. It paid off – all those shares by the student-athletes led to explosive growth on our Instagram account. Why? Remember what I said in the section on metrics: whenever people share your content, you're getting it put in front of people who don't follow you.

This Instagram example is especially a good example of knowing your audience and how they are using the platform. Every piece of social media best practice literature at the time said to prioritize video – and we had video segments of the athletes to post. But when we experimented, we found that the athletes wanted to see a photo of themselves, and were more likely to share a cool graphic featuring

them in their stories versus a video where it
was harder to pick them out of the team.
And that leads us into our next step.

Chapter 7

Get to Know What Your Audience Wants, What They Really, Really Want

Maybe the most crucial point to take out of everything I wrote in the last chapter: If we hadn't spent the time to try different things, to test and retest and analyze the results, and to spend time within the platform itself and observe behavior, we wouldn't have had the success we did.

That last sentence brings up an important point, so important that I'm going to give it its own line:

There is no such thing as a content failure, only data.

You worked hard on a post and it flopped? Don't blame yourself, your audience, or the algorithm.

I mean, you can, but it's a waste of your time.

Just look for the insights it gives you and apply them to the next piece of content you work on. Why did it flop? Was it the format (i.e. video versus graphic versus photo)? Was it the copy? Try to look at it with an objective eye. If you didn't have any vested interest in it, would you pay any attention to it? Would it stop your scrolling? If not, what would? Go back to the drawing board and try again. That's how you get to the next step.

Step three: Figure out what your audience wants – both in general, and on a specific platform. This is Step Two drilled down to figure out patterns. Let's work through an example of this.

Where is my audience, and what is their behavior on that platform?

Let's say your target audience is on TikTok, and they're creating and responding to a lot of videos that use humor and trending sounds.

What does that tell you?

Your audience is hungry for entertainment, and they like the feeling of being in on a joke. At the same time, they get bored and will move on from a meme (meaning a shared joke) pretty rapidly. A sound that was trending six months ago would probably no longer feel relevant to them.

What do they want?

To succeed with this audience, your content had better make them laugh. I would argue that you could potentially also aim for content that will make your audience cry or get angry. The key is that it should make them feel something and give them a momentary escape. They want a sense of being in on a joke, and while they won't tolerate you using a trend beyond its time, they will embrace a highly specific inside joke that you create *with* them and keep revisiting. (*See also*: Duolingo's obsession with singer and name doppelganger Dua Lipa.) They value cleverness and wit over high production values. They'd rather see something you moved quickly on to be relevant than something that had to go through rounds of approvals and is no longer of the moment.

Here is where knowing what your target audience wants, expects, and responds to on a specific platform needs to guide your social strategy. It's easy to get bogged down in content creation that has multiple layers of oversight, feedback, and checks and re-checks. That can be a death sentence for this type of content. While you certainly want to do your due diligence and avoid putting out sloppy or poorly thought out content, having too many cooks in the content kitchen is a recipe for some weak-ass sauce. Avoid at all costs. If you are lucky enough to work with social media professionals, listen to them. Protect their ability to stay nimble and responsive, even when it scares you a little bit. (If it scares you, challenge them to talk to you about the strategy behind what they're doing! If they can't, buy them a copy of this book.)

*

It's also helpful to get an idea of what your audience responds to on a more macro scale. Here are my own generalizations I keep in mind when thinking through strategy. I know these are very broad strokes, even stereotypes, but they can also help me as I think through online behavior.

Baby Boomers (1946 – 1964) and Gen X (1965– 1980): want *information* and *connection*. This is why they're still heavily using Facebook. This is why, I would argue, they can fall victim to misinformation on that platform. This is why they will comment on everyyyyyythingggg. Reaching them is all about helping them feel informed and/or part of a community. If you can do either of those things – or better yet, both – then you win.

Millennials (1981– 1996) want *authenticity*. While they were responsible for the rise of the influencer, they are also part of the influencer's downfall. They're over it. They're savvy, and they know that the influencer du jour who is touting a product may or may not be genuine in their reviews, especially if they are a celebrity.

Gen Z (1997– 2012) wants the same authenticity that Millennials want – but turned up to 11.[5] As of this writing (2024), they are increasingly turning to microinfluencers, or a more organic form of reviews like "get ready with me"/GRWM videos, or even "deinfluencing" (which is, in itself, influencing). If Gen Z smells even a whiff of marketing, they're turned off – or worse, they will actively fight against it. (An interesting example of these mental gymnastics: they are turning away from the influencer trend but have steadily replaced it with "creators." Whether that is truly different in any notable way remains to be seen.) A love of the raw, imperfect, and unpredictable is why Gen Z has picked up disposable cameras and indeed, film photography itself. You'll notice that their media seems less refined – forget highly

---

[5]For those of you who aren't Gen X, that was a *Spinal Tap* reference. I apologize for both the reference and this footnote.

polished Instagram feeds that fit a certain aesthetic just so. If you look at a photo carousel from them, expect to see a mix of flattering photos and goofy/random/candid ones.

Finally – and forgive me for writing the most about this generation, but they truly fascinate me – Gen Z is one of the most politically active ones we've seen at a young age since the Boomers in their hippie, antiwar era. This generation has been raised differently, both on- and offline, and speaking up for their political beliefs online comes naturally to them. You see this most often with the social-justice-oriented among them. They're not afraid to express their beliefs or to push for change – and they expect the same from the people and brands they follow online. So, a word to the wise with Gen Z: mess with their sense of authenticity – or indeed, social justice – at your own peril.

CASE STUDY: "Tramp Stamps" band

Being an "industry plant" or manufactured pop group[6] is nothing new. The Monkees, the Spice Girls, 'NSYNC and The Backstreet Boys all found major fame and commercial success despite lacking hardscrabble origin stories.

You would forgive music executives in the 2020s for assuming that it was pretty much business as usual when they assembled a new, all-female pop punk act. It was three youngish (no shade! We are going to get to the -*ish* part in a second) women, all with their hair dyed a different jewel tone, playing songs with a perfect blend of edge and palatability.

One of their first releases featured the lyric "I'd rather die/rather die than sleep with another straight white guy."

You could almost see the music execs rubbing their hands with glee and high-fiving. How could this NOT go viral?

---

[6] Okay, yes, those two terms are not at all the same. BUT the terms are used interchangeably among outraged Gen Z'ers online, which we're about to get into. Just hold on, okay! Stop coming down to my footnotes to argue with me!

Here's a lesson we all need to learn right now: sometimes things can go viral for the wrong reasons.

Another social media lesson, and something we saw with Duolingo's initial TikTok presence: it's possible to be SO CLOSE and yet not quite there.

In this case, the band – which the label (I assume) named "Tramp Stamps," did indeed start to get attention, mostly with Gen Z on TikTok and Reddit.

And it wasn't good.

The label launched the band with what I would presume is their usual playbook, releasing the band into the social media sphere with a few songs (including the one with the cringey lyric above), a back story (they were friends who met and bonded blah blah blah) and a conveniently search-engine-optimized website.

But Gen Z. Gen Z was not amused. And Tramp Stamps, unfortunately, went the way of real-life tramp stamps – quickly becoming something that can never be completely scrubbed away but will forever try to be hidden.

The first issue was the name. If you're trying to target Gen Z, you might not want to use a name that . . . doesn't really have meaning to them. Tramp Stamps (aka a tattoo at the small of your back that peeks out over the top of low-rise jeans) are an early-aughts thing. A MILLENNIAL thing. And Millennial things, to Gen Z, are EW.

Then there was that song lyric, which seemed a bit off to Gen Z. I guess it was meant to be something funny, something girls say to their girlfriends when they've had another bad date, right? Har har. But somehow it just rang false. Maybe it was the venom with which it was sung. It just seemed a bit – performative. Inauthentic. And it seemed to commodify, if not outright mock, the queer community. So the Gen Z TikTokers who were already suspicious of Tramp Stamps did something they are naturally very good at: internet sleuthing. In their deep digging into the group, they found that the drummer was, in fact, MARRIED. To a white guy.

She was also clearly ... not Gen Z. They gleefully started sharing photos of her and her husband, looking perfectly happy and goofy and millennial and straight, and it was just more proof for their final verdict: Tramp Stamps was FAKE. In the words of many a commentator on TikTok and Reddit: they were an INDUSTRY PLANT.

For Gen Z, there were plenty of other reasons to dislike and distrust them, all discussed at length in the hundreds of TikTok videos and Reddit posts on the topic, of course. Creators found information about the group members' past careers. Creators dissected their website and production style. They discussed their backstory and how it was or wasn't believable.

In the end, the kids weren't buying it.

And in the end, Tramp Stamps couldn't overcome the negativity, and bowed out of the spotlight in 2021.

*

CASE STUDY: The Kyle Scheele Meal

A more minor and regional backlash happened when an influencer named Kyle Scheele managed to fanboy his way into getting a named meal at Kum & Go[7]. The story, as chronicled in a series of TikToks, was that Kyle Scheele placed a life-sized cardboard cutout of himself in his local Kum & Go to advertise the "Kyle Scheele Meal." The videos of the prank proved to be so popular that Kum & Go relented and created a Kyle Scheele Meal, for real. Pretty cool, huh?

Except. The whole thing was preplanned. Honestly, it was a clever and original influencer collaboration – if not totally honest. However, what Kum & Go didn't count on was how much backlash they'd get when their Gen Z audience – who loved Kum & Go's otherwise Gen Z-friendly social media presence – would react to being bamboozled. *"You liiiiiiied to us!"* you could almost hear the collective wailing. It wasn't a pretty look – either for the youths publishing videos complaining about being duped by a gas station named Kum & Go, or for the company.

---

[7] For those of you who don't live in a very specific portion of the Midwest: Kum & Go is the very real name of a chain of gas stations that, unfortunately, were recently bought out by Maverik.

Kyle Scheele seems to have emerged from the controversy unscathed, however. As of August 2024, he still has three million TikTok followers, so, you know, he's doing alright.

Chapter 8

Bringing a Dash of Cold, Hard Reality into It

Alright. Now you know who you want to reach (your audience), where they're hanging out (the social media platforms), and what their general behavior and expectations are (the tactics). By now, your brain might be buzzing with all the possibilities for things you could do. Our next step, however, is to take a breath and look at things with a realistic eye.

Step four: evaluate your brand's a) capacity for additional workload and b) tolerance for risk.

Social media is a hungry beast that can eat up your time very quickly. It's easy to get carried away and want to be on every platform, jumping on every trend, and imitating every cool thing you see other accounts doing. Unfortunately, that's the fast path to burnout, scope creep (things expanding beyond the original plan) and frustration, among other things.

You need to take a hard, honest look at how much support you/your social media team has. Are you working with designers and copywriters, or are you doing all creative yourself? Do you have a full team with specialists, strategists, and a social media manager to work on your social media, or are you just a small business owner who's trying to fit things in among all the other things you have to do to run your business? The answers to these questions matter.

At the same time, you also need to be realistic about how "out there" you're willing to get. What makes sense for your brand? (And if your brand is you – that's still a brand.)

When I started my career in social media, a leader told me that using gifs would be "out there" for our brand. I thought they were wrong, but I had to respect their vision for what our brand should look like online..

But that's something that no one told young Amanda – that a corporate brand in a buttoned-up, regulated industry is going to be slower to respond to online trends, no matter how good you think they are. I could have saved myself a lot of frustration and heartache if I had understood our brand's tolerance for risk/change and adjusted my expectations and plans accordingly. I'm not saying I would never have suggested new and exciting things, but I would have done it more strategically. There's no use dying on a hill for a tactic that doesn't make sense for your brand when you could save your energy spending time on things that will truly move the needle for your brand.

Let's say the buck stops with you – you're the one who is responsible for determining your brand's tolerance for risk. How do you figure out what the sweet spot for you is? Well – and you're probably going to turn me saying this into a drinking game – but it depends. It all comes back to what makes sense for your marketing goals, as well as what you honestly have the capacity to do.

It's better to do a few platforms well than to be on ALL of them but executing poorly. No one sets out to do that on purpose, of course, but it ends up happening because you don't have the time and capacity. TikTok, for example, always looks easy and fun – but anyone who has tried to make a "quick TikTok" knows how time-consuming it can be! Another example is going live on a platform. They can be a very effective way to grow an audience – but there's a lot you can't control, which is scary for some brands with low risk tolerance.

Again, I'm not saying you should never push boundaries or do new and innovative things on social media. I'm saying do it only where it makes sense for your goals, your audience, your brand and your staff capacity – whether that's you or a team you manage. Often, the social media team is one of the smallest teams in a department. They're always being asked to do a lot with little, which is all the more reason to focus efforts. Don't burn a team out – or allow yourself to get burned out.

When you're thinking about bandwidth and risk tolerance, it's a good time to think about community-building and customer service. It's a crucial part of your social media presence, but it can end up eating up your time. A lot of people make it an afterthought, but it's better to plan right away. Consider: Will you respond to comments? Private/direct messages? Which ones? Why? (If I haven't established this already, it's always good to be able to articulate the *why* for these decisions.)

For example: When we were building the social media presence at the telecommunications company, I started my social media career at, we made a policy to respond to every comment. EVERY. COMMENT. Why? Because people generally see their ISP/cable company as coldly corporate, uncaring, greedy – any number of negative adjectives. By responding to people's thoughts and concerns, especially publicly, we strove to change that image. It paid off: our company was recognized by J.D. Power for exceptional customer service, in part due to our social media customer care team.

When you think about customer care and community building, think through these considerations:

- Who will do the responding? Is it the job of the social media team, or do you have a separate customer care team? What is your system for elevating concerns? What is your plan for training whoever will be responding – both on how to do it, but also on all the things they need to know to be able to provide support and build community?

- What is your voice going to be? Do you want whoever is responding as your brand to sound like YOUR BRAND, or is there room for a little personality?

At the telecom I worked at, I trained our digital customer care team to use one brand voice, but allowed them to insert their own tone – dependent upon both the situation and their personality. We had an agent who was prone to dad jokes, and I encouraged him to go ahead and make them – because it fit in with the strategy I described earlier to humanize and warm up the brand.

It's worth thinking through the little details, like whether or not you or your team uses emojis and gifs, and if you sign off with their name when responding, or if you want to simply act as the brand. Going back to the telecom, I had agents sign off with their first name (or a pseudonym, if they wanted privacy). This helped humanize the brand online and reminded customers that they were dealing with a real person online – not a faceless ISP that hiked their monthly bill and ticked them off.

Chapter 9

When and How to Spend Your Money

The biggest matchup of our time isn't in sports. It isn't in politics, either.

It's organic vs. paid efforts – ie., putting money behind your social media efforts with ads and boosts or not.

It's been in vogue lately to say that organic social is dead. Even writing that makes me laugh – it's been in vogue for the last ten years to say that organic social is dead.

I am here to assure you that it is not. It is just not as easy as it was at the birth of every new platform (Facebook, Instagram, Twitter, TikTok…the list goes on and on). At some point, the market gets saturated, there's a lot of noise, and you can't command attention just by *existing*.

The high school homecoming queen has to go to college and experience being just another face in the crowd. Sorry. It happens. You can bitch and moan about the glory days, or you can embrace it as a chance to learn, change, and *pivot*. Which sounds more exciting to you?

If it's the latter, you might as well stop reading this book now. Sorry. No refunds.

But if you'd rather watch a movie or read a story about a washed-up football star or high school homecoming queen who discovers a whole new and exciting way of existing in this big ol' world, then hang tight. That's exactly where we're going.

Organic platforms can and do still pull massive numbers and do incredible amounts of work for people and businesses every day.

But, I would wager, the people running those accounts are savvy. They are looking at what's working, what their audience wants, blah blah blah – everything I talked about in the previous chapters.

It's also fashionable in some circles to say, "Well, it's all pay to play these days, so you just have to throw money at your social media efforts."

I have bad news for you.

If your post sucks, it sucks. It doesn't matter how much money you throw behind it.

With that said, there is a place for both organic and paid social media in your efforts. And how much you focus on each effort depends largely on a) your budget and b) what you're trying to accomplish.

Figuring out the right mix between paid and organic efforts is the bane of many a senior-level marketer and the nuances are too many for me to list here. However, I can give you some points to consider.

- If your budget is low, focus on good, sharable organic content. Heck, you should be focusing on this anyway. In the social media world, it's rare to find high-performing paid content that wouldn't also work well as organic content.

- Focus your organic efforts on building brand awareness and affinity, and your paid efforts on driving specific actions, like clicking on a link to buy, signing up for your email list, etc. The reason for this is that most platforms' paid services, like Facebook Ads Manager, for example, can help you maximize your ads for action-oriented goals to get the most out of your dollars.

- Think of your organic efforts as scaffolding for your paid efforts. Or, think of it as a pyramid. Your organic efforts are the base: broad, wide, far-reaching, not overly targeted. Your paid efforts are the top: pointed, targeted, narrow, leading toward a specific action.

- Don't fall into the temptation of going "spray and pray" for your paid creative – using one single piece of creative for your TV ad, your YouTube preroll ad, and your Facebook story ad. All three of these placements have different creative needs, not to mention different audiences.

If I'm starting to get too into the weeds for you, it might be best to a) partner with a freelancer or agency on paid efforts or b) focus your efforts on one or two platforms that you can take the time to learn and understand well. I personally advocate starting out with advertising on Meta, because a) you can place ads on Facebook, Instagram, and Messenger, reaching a wide range of people, and b) once you master their advertising interface, the other platforms' ads managers are fairly easy to learn.

Chapter 10

Partnering with Influencers

In all this talk about paid versus organic social media, the topic of influencers invariably comes up. Whether it's a post-for-post agreement with a local microinfluencer, an NIL[8] deal with a college athlete, or a partnership with a big-name influencer with a seven-digit follower count, there's no denying that working with actual people to help spread the word

---

[8] Name, Image, Likeness. "In the simplest of terms, Name, Image and Likeness (NIL) is a term that describes the means through which college athletes are allowed to receive financial compensation. NIL refers to the use of an athlete's name, image, and likeness through marketing and promotional endeavors. This can include autograph signings, product endorsements, social media posts, and more." -iconsource.com

about your brand or products can be a great
marketing strategy.

However, there are a few things you should
keep in mind when you consider working with
influencers.

- How will you measure success/ROI
  (return on investment)? Will it be
  impressions, or will you give them some
  kind of promo code? Who will be
  responsible for measuring/reporting it?

- How much editorial control will you have
  over the content they post on your
  behalf? Will there be an approval/review
  process before they post sponsored
  content?

- Can you include a contractual clause
  that allows you to end the contract if
  their other content is damaging to your
  brand? It only takes one drunk
  Instagram story before you start to
  regret your association with an
  individual.

- How much content will you ask for? Will it be in the form of stories (24 hours only) or feed posts? Will they have to tag you (hint: YES)? If posts on the feed/grid, do they need to stay up indefinitely, or can the influencer delete them at some point?

- How will you compensate them? Will it be money, product, or a post for post type deal?

- What is the scope of your relationship? Is it an amount of time, number of posts, or reaching a certain key performance indicator (KPI) such as number of impressions?

- How can the content be used by the influencer? By you? Is there any expectation for sharing on either side?

- How often and through what mediums should professional communication

happen? You may want to set a
baseline for check-ins to ensure that
neither side feels as though they are
being ghosted.

Chapter 11

Getting Help

At some point, your accounts will grow to the point – or they may already be there! – where you realize you need help. Never fear; help is to be had.

One of the biggest things people find helpful is converting from publishing natively (i.e., within the platform itself – so logging in to Facebook, Instagram, etc. to post) to using a third-party platform. There are a number of options at various price points and capabilities. There are a few things to be clear on as you start your research:

- Do you want scheduling and publishing, social listening, or responding and customer care capabilities? Or do you want all three?

- What is your price point?

- What is the tool's pricing structure? Is it per user, per month with unlimited seats/users, or something else?

- What social accounts do you need to be able to publish to? Different publishing tools are better for different social media platforms. Some of the most well-established tools, like Hootsuite, can publish to most of the mainstream social media platforms. Others specialize in one or two – Instagram or Snapchat, for example.

- Do you need/want your tool to have collaboration tools? What about an approval process?

- Do you need your tool to serve as a drive/asset manager to save your creative files?

- How detailed do you need the analytics to be? What do you need reports to look like?

Since tools change so rapidly, I won't name a lot of companies or write much about details. I will say that at the time of this writing (2024), I feel two of the best and most robust social media tools are Hootsuite and Khoros. Hootsuite wins for social listening and reporting, and Khoros wins for scalable customer care. They are about equal in terms of publishing capabilities. Pricing on both platforms varies depending on a few variables including the number of users you have and number of solutions you have (customer care, social listening, robust analytics, etc).

The best thing to do as you begin looking for a tool is to think about the considerations I've outlined above and use that to inform your search. Maybe you just want something to help you publish to Instagram? That will be a totally different search – and discovery process – than if you need an all-in-one tool like Hootsuite or Khoros.

All in all, when in doubt, underbuy – go with a skinnier tool with the features you know you need and can use, and you can always upgrade down the road. Even with the most comprehensive tool, the odds are you will still have to do some things natively. The tools' capabilities are dependent upon their connections with the social platforms, and unfortunately, those don't update as fast as new features come out.

Chapter 12

Getting More Help

At some point, you may consider working with an external partner, like a digital agency or freelancers, to support your social media efforts. This can be an expensive prospect, so it's wise to weigh the pros and cons carefully. While I've personally only worked in-house and freelance, I've worked alongside freelancers and agencies enough to give you some idea of the considerations you need to take into account.

Pricing: While agency costs are notoriously high, they can range wildly depending on the size of the agency and the market you are in. On the other hand, companies are often attracted to freelancers because they are perceived to be cheaper than full-time staff – even if they have a higher hourly wage, they usually aren't entitled to benefits.

Subject matter expertise: No matter how good your relationship with an agency or freelancer is, in general, they will not have the same subject matter expertise and institutional knowledge that an in-house employee has. They aren't part of the same conversations, both informal and informal, that inform choices. There's also the additional difficulty of getting them access to the internal systems they may need to do their job – things such as drives, digital asset managers, etc. These hurdles can be overcome, but companies in especially data-sensitive or highly regulated industries, like health and financial, may want to take that into consideration.

Creative chops: There is an aura around agencies that the quality of creative work you can get from them is better than what you get from in-house staff. I have seen mixed results. On one hand, some agencies tend to hire employees straight out of college, flush with fresh ideas and the latest and greatest education. On the other hand, in-house employees often have a surplus of work and sometimes feel constrained by brand or creative restrictions. Freelancers can run the gamut – from fresh out of school to very experienced – but you will pay accordingly. Whichever you choose, make sure you get a portfolio so you can see with your own eyes the kind of work they produce.

Influencers as freelancers: If a freelancer you are interviewing has a sizable social following of their own, make sure their portfolios include work they have done on behalf of other entities or brands. Creating a social platform for yourself, when your looks, personality, style or knowledge is the draw, is quite different than creating a social platform for a company or business brand – which may not be nearly as sexy or fun as a personal brand.

LOE (Level of Effort) for you: How much time do you have to train, communicate, and proof work? The time spent training freelancers, plus preparing work for them, can add up, especially in the beginning. However, collaboration with a well-trained and long-term freelancer can be no more difficult than working with a part-time or offsite employee.

Security: Remember that every person who has access to your account puts it at risk. This is especially true for platforms like Facebook or LinkedIn, which connect users' personal accounts to the brand accounts they work on. If someone connected to your social fails to take security measures such as using a strong password and turning on two-factor authentication, they put your brand account in danger of being compromised. Regaining control of a hacked account can be a long, frustrating process, and you may not even be successful.

This is a big selling point for those third-party social media tools like Hootsuite and

Khoros; they can allow multiple team members to work on an account without sharing a password or using their own social accounts. This is especially handy if you're working in for a company that might need a lot of team members or different teams for inbound (messages, comments) and/or outbound (publishing posts). Depending on your business, you may benefit from having a dedicated digital customer support team that works only with inbound social. In those cases, I strongly recommend using a tool for security, not to mention analytics and management of the customer care queue.

Chapter 13

It's Like Premarital Counseling, but For Your Content Partnership

Whether it's with a freelancer, an intern, an agency, or an influencer, if you are working with a third party on your social media efforts, there are steps you can take to ensure success.

The first and most obvious is to share your goals. If you have a content or platform brief, share it. If you have a strategy for your platform or campaign (and if you don't – please reread this book), make sure you review it with them. What I like to say is, you don't have to build out the whole road, but at least show them where you want to get. Define what success looks like. Your social partner's job is to figure out what they can do to help you get from point A to point B. Sharing your strategy with your social partner helps them know how to best get you there.

CASE STUDY: Account Management Professionals of Northeast Iowa

The trade group Insurance Management Professionals of Northeast Iowa[9] wanted to start an Instagram account, but their volunteer social media manager had to go on medical leave. They began working with an intern who was a college-aged social media influencer, but conflict soon broke out among the executive team about the direction and tone of social posts. They all agreed they wanted to be funny and edgy to appeal to a younger demographic but disagreed on whether the sarcastic memes and reels the intern created were appropriate. Were the jokes liable to

---

[9] Not a real group (that I know of) – but this is a very real case study.

harm their message? Could they turn off their target audience or hurt relationships with key business partners?

In talking to them, I found that the president was setting the direction for the account and coming up with content ideas, and then the intern was executing and posting without any further oversight. I advised them to move away from this system by implementing a simple review/approval process. I also advised them to take the time to create a one-page strategic brief for their Instagram account that would help the marketing committee of the executive board govern the new platform. At a minimum, this brief should list:

Their primary goal (drive engagement among current members? Drive sign-ups of new members? Drive registration to events?) **and any secondary goals** (brand awareness, etc.).

The target audience (again, remembering that "everyone" is not an audience!). For this account, I advised focusing on new graduates and early-career insurance management professionals. What does this target audience care about? What kind of content are they interacting with? What are their online and offline habits and behaviors? This may take some formal and informal research, but if you start with broad generational assumptions like "Gen Z," there is a wealth of information online.

Key messages: They should align with your goal(s), of course.

Content pillars: What topics will you talk about? Remember, you want to talk about things that are both relevant to your goals AND your audience's interests. Identify a few main themes or topics around which content will be created (e.g., educational, promotional, behind-the-scenes).

Content selection: what kinds of content will you focus on? Even if you are focused on one platform, such as Instagram, there is a wealth of options. For this example, they may want to focus on organic carousels, reels, and stories for the day-to-day content, and paid stories for bigger events and membership drives.

Metrics: How will they measure success on this platform? The answer to this will go back to their goals in the first bullet.

Ideally, their brief should also include thoughts on the following:

Engagement plan: Social media is still social. How will you engage with your audience? Will you respond to their comments and questions? What about DMs on this new platform? Who will be responsible for that? Do you have a process for escalating any sensitive issues that may come up?

Budget: Do they want to spend any money boosting their posts on this platform? If so, they should note the budget, timeline, and a high-level outline of the boosting cadence (e.g. only during certain special events/times of year? Monthly?).

Amanda F. Potter

Chapter 14

Say It with Your Chest. Or Not.

Earlier, I mentioned training a customer care
team on voice (think: company-wide) and tone
(think: personal and situational, like the agent
who made dad jokes). I think it's worth
exploring voice and tone more, because the
place it really shines is social media. A
distinctive voice and tone is what makes
companies like Wendy's, Oatly, Slack, Skittles
and Dove stand out from the pack with their
social media accounts.

You'll notice that I just listed five very
different examples. While Wendy's is sarcastic
on X, Dove goes all-in on earnestness. Your

brand's voice on social media can be whatever you want it to be, but the point is: it should be *something*.

My friend Denise DePaolo[10], who is a brilliant writer, editor, and PR and communications professional, says she likes to think about your social voice as being like your brand's personal style. Your tone is like your outfit. If it's raining, snowing, or 85 degrees, you're going to dress accordingly. That's the tone. But your voice is your overall style – i.e. preppy, classic, casual, boho, minimalist, or tomboy. If you have a defined sense of style, your clothing will vary depending on the context of your day (JUST LIKE YOUR TONE, if you're not following the metaphor here), but you're going to stay within the same general style. If you choose to break your style – if you usually dress in a tomboy style and suddenly wear a feminine, ruffled, flowery dress – people might be confused. At the same time, it can be a very effective way to grab attention or make a statement – it's just something that should be

---

[10] Find Denise on LinkedIn under Denise (Orton) DePaolo.

used sparingly, lest you come across as a bit unhinged. A personal style – and, following the analogy, a brand voice – that varies wildly can come across as untrustworthy; disingenuous. People like to know what to expect, and giving consumers a clear idea of who you are via voice and tone builds trust.

If you don't know what your brand voice is or should be, there are any number of exercises online. Denise's method is to come up with three adjectives to define the brand and work from there – much the way you might with your personal style. So if your style words are tomboy, sporty, and casual, you would go all-in on athleisure and might pair your business suits with an endless rotation of high-end sneakers. Similarly, if your brand voice is warm, engaging, and friendly, you might think about keeping your copy between a sixth- and eighth-grade reading level – higher reading levels seem more formal – and include lots of nice "filler" works like "absolutely." Don't believe me? Look at the difference between these two responses to a customer request for help via social media:

Customer: "Hi! My internet is down. Can you help?"

NO: "Yes. Have you tried unplugging your modem, waiting 60 seconds, and plugging it back in again?"

YES: "Sure! I can absolutely help you out today. Let's cross a few easy troubleshooting steps off the list first ..."

Your tone may well vary by platform, since your audiences, their needs, and your goals all may differ by platform. It's like the old meme that showed different pictures of a person, supposedly from different social media platforms: in a suit for LinkedIn. Hugging grandma for Facebook. Doing a kegstand for Instagram. All different photos – ALL THE SAME PERSON. Mind blown, right? Okay, maybe not. We understand that we all present slightly different sides of ourselves depending on the context of different social media platforms. Well, that's exactly what differentiating your tone slightly by platform does for your brand. Remember – voice largely stays the same. Tone changes.

Chapter 15

How to Deal with the Bad Vibes

I have to have a word with you about the haters.

You are going to get negative comments. That's the way social media works. And your first impulse is going to be to hide or delete them. That's normal.

I want you to take a beat before you do that, though.

First of all, take a breath and send some good vibes to the haters, because they're giving you some almighty engagement. I'm not trying to be flippant, because yes, negative comments can truly damage your brand, and besides that, they suck to read. But – it does still help your algorithmic ranking and gets more eyeballs on your content.

Next, let's think about this strategically. When deciding what to do with negative comments, I like to employ a two-part rubric:

- Is it untrue/spreading misinformation?
- Is it offensive or potentially harmful for others (e.g., minors) to see?

I use my answers to these questions to guide my decisions – yes, even over potential impact to the brand.

First things first. If your brand has the potential for getting lots of negative comments, then you may want to consider putting your own "terms of service" in your "About" section on certain platforms. Consider wording like, "We welcome your comments and feedback, but any offensive, inaccurate, or inappropriate remarks may be removed to maintain a respectful and positive community."

Secondly, on Facebook, there are two different ways to deal with undesirable comments. There is a "delete" option, of course, but there is also a "hide" option. The "delete" button can be a bit of a nuclear option for someone who is emotionally charged. They will feel like you are censoring them, limiting their ability to give feedback, etc. The "hide" button hides the comment from public views except from the person who left it and their friends. Therefore, it is viewable to a much smaller (hopefully) group of people, and the commenter is unaware that you've moderated their response. I find this to be a much more effective tool.

Many social platforms have filters you can set up that will censor or automatically hide comments that use objectionable language, if you want to ensure that your accounts stay family friendly. Third-party tools often have similar filters to do the work for you.

Blocking someone from your page, of course, is also an option, but not an action I would advise except for the most extreme cases.

CASE STUDY: Foundational posts

A nonprofit reached out to me for advice on how to deal with a lot of criticism they were dealing with online. They had recently changed the structure of their fundraiser so that it benefited a larger group of children instead of one narrowly defined group. The parents of the children who had previously benefited from the fundraiser were vocal in their outrage over the change, posting on their own accounts as well as the nonprofit's posts on its Facebook page.

The nonprofit had been deleting the posts, which only seemed to anger the parents further, causing them to call for others to boycott this nonprofit and its fundraiser. I advised the nonprofit to take the following steps.

1. Create a post talking about the change to the fundraiser, including the larger group of recipients, in the most positive way possible. Emphasize the good (i.e., that this would now help more children). Allow people to post their thoughts and feelings there, as is perfectly

appropriate. Respond to comments publicly and empathetically, with an invitation to visit the nonprofit's office and talk to someone in person about the changes.

This response was strategic. I wanted the nonprofit to show anyone looking at their page that they were listening to their donors, but that they could not be bullied. I knew that people who complain online typically will not take further action and complain in person (or via a phone call) – but if they did, that would be the nonprofit's opportunity to turn a hater into an advocate.

2. Stop deleting negative comments on non-fundraiser-related posts, because it was just feeding into the negativity. Instead, use the "hide" function.

3. Make sure all posts about the fundraiser use images and stories about the children benefiting from it (with fully documented permission, of course!).

Few people have the *cajones* to go off on a post featuring a sweet child who needs funds for his or her medical treatment. And if they do, they are the ones who end up looking bad – so let them.

"Isn't that kind of throwing these kids and their families to the wolves?" the marketing team from the nonprofit wondered. That's a valid concern. I advised them to let the parents of the featured children know about the situation up front and make a fully informed decision about whether they wanted their children featured.

In the end, the nonprofit ended up implementing most of my suggestions, and while they still received criticism online, it didn't keep their fundraiser from being a success – benefiting more children than ever.

Chapter 16

It's Your Sandbox

The biggest advice I can give you is don't count yourself out.

What do I mean by that?

I mean that platform X may prioritize video. That's what the prevailing wisdom says, anyway. But your brand excels in photo content. *That's it,* you think. *I'll never be able to excel on this platform.*

Don't. Count. Yourself. Out.

Remember what I said earlier: no failure, only data. Yes, that's a bit of an oversimplification – you could accidentally post a photo of your drunken night out to a corporate account, and that is objectively a failure – but broadly speaking, when a piece of content underperforms, you can't think of it as a loss. All it is, is data. Is it the content? Are you failing to interest your audience? If so, what is it about the content? Is it the copy, the creative, or both? Or is it the time of day? The format? The placement? Social media is a game of testing and retesting. The only way you will find success is by continually taking the time to analyze what you've done and why it performed the way it did.

At the time of this writing, the prevailing wisdom for Facebook is this: video is king, and people don't have the attention spans for long captions. But the *Humans of New York* account has found success with photos and long-form content that sometimes spreads out over multiple posts.

Yes, you need to know what is trending and what is typically working well on platforms, what algorithms are rewarding, etc. But you also need to test and evaluate what is working for your account and your audience.

At the same time, don't be quick to blame your performance woes on the platforms. Keeping up with nebulous algorithmic changes is a challenge to be sure, especially when the platforms are less than transparent about them. But by and large, I find accounts and creators who blame poor post performance on the platforms – and use it as an opportunity to ask for more likes and comments – a bit lazy. Is it the platform, or is it your content? Social is a world that is always changing, and what worked yesterday may not work today. That's the fun and the frustration of it.

Chapter 17

Remember Your Website?
She Misses You!

By now, if you weren't already, you might be all in on your social media strategy. I hope so, anyway. But now is a good time to pull on the reins a bit, though, and remind you: you don't own your social media platforms.

Sure, I know it feels like it. You spend so much time curating your audience, your content, your profile. But the reality is that any given platform that you're on could shut down suddenly, taking your audience and all your content with it. Keep that in mind as you work on an overall content strategy. It's like being a homeowner – you should have some kind of insurance. In this case, what is that insurance? Diversification and owned platforms.

Diversification: make sure you are not putting your eggs all in one basket. Despite what I said earlier in this section, it's a good idea to be on at least two platforms, so you have a backup if things go south on one of them. Again, I don't advise putting time and effort into platforms that don't make sense for your goals, audience, and bandwidth. But the classic social combo of Facebook + X works for many companies for a reason – you can curate different audiences, but you also have backup accounts. If X starts to get weird (I'm looking at you, Elon), you aren't starting over from scratch. Might you jump to another platform to try to capture the same audience you had there? Sure, but at least you aren't completely without a social presence – or with a dysfunctional social presence – while you figure out what your next steps are.

The next step in your personal content strategy insurance is investing in your owned platforms. This is your website or blog. On these platforms, you have full control over your content – the limits to what you can post on these platforms are largely self-imposed. You have more power to shape your brand image, messaging, and user experience to be exactly the way you want it to be. You're also not fighting an algorithm – you're fighting for visibility and search engine goodness, which is a different challenge. Unlike social media platforms that can and do change their algorithms or platform experience seemingly on a whim, without so much as a notification to you, the user, your website and blog offer a stable foundation to showcase your brand.

Chapter 18

PR + Communication + Social = The Ultimate Power of Throuple

Unless you are an entrepreneur or a team of one, social media and PR/Comms are often different roles. Increasingly, though, they are roles that have to work hand-in-hand. It makes sense, right? Social is where people go for information, for breaking news. In my career, I've been part of the comms team and the digital marketing teams. I've found that I have to be *thisclose* to my partners on the external comms and PR side, aligning with them on messaging and helping them understand best practices for posting on social media (as well as, you know, putting up posts for them!).

This relationship is critical during crisis communications, which I will talk about in depth in a moment. However, since you know that your socials are dependent upon algorithms, a smart marketer learns to use social to build engagement and sentiment before a crisis ever hits. A smart marketer also creates a crisis comms plan for social now, before, as they say, SHTF[11]. Having social media as part of your crisis comms plan before a crisis even occurs is crucial for brands in today's digital landscape. The immediacy and amplification of society can move both positive and negative information at warp speed. By proactively developing your plan for how you will utilize the platform, you can effectively manage and mitigate the impact of a crisis, protecting your brand reputation and maintaining public trust. A well-prepared plan allows brands to respond swiftly, maintain transparency, and provide accurate information in a crisis.

Your plan should include the nitty-gritty of when and how you will post, as well as clear guidelines for the tone, messaging, and timing. Planning ahead will also allow you to get messaging out quickly, which is critical during a

---

[11]Shit hits the fan. Hi, mom!

crisis comms situation. Social media can be one of the biggest factors in controlling the narrative and sentiment during a time of crisis. And if you don't control the narrative, you're leaving it up to others to do so – namely the public and the press.

Speaking of the press – with traditional news media struggling for funding and cutting staff left and right, I'm seeing more and more news outlets use a brand's social media as a source for their reporting. I've personally had comments that I made to customers through the brand account quoted as official company statements. Does that terrify you? It should. That's exactly why social, PR and comms need to be aligned, especially when a crisis occurs.

Part of your social crisis comms plan should be a strategy for how you will deal (or not deal) with incoming comments and messages. Will you answer all of them? Just some? Only public ones, or only private ones? Will you direct public ones to go to private? Who will be responding to messages, and who will help craft talking points for responses? If you need to increase staff to deal with a sudden increase in volume, how will you do so? (This is especially important for service-oriented brands!) If you have contingency plans for adding extra "hands on deck" to help you with an increase in incoming messages, do you have a way to quickly give them access – either by adding them to your third-party platform, like Hootsuite, or by giving them native access? These details seem like they'll be easy enough to figure out in the moment, but trust me: when everything else is going haywire, you'll be glad to have a clear plan of how you will handle it all.

Something else to consider is how you will handle trauma and burnout to employees after a crisis. Dealing with person after person messaging you who is angry, sad, confused, scared, and may be taking it all out on you is hard even on the most seasoned social media professional. At the very least, it's good to let employees know that it's normal to have different feelings after guiding a brand through a crisis comms situation. You may feel energized, burned out, depressed, or traumatized. It's important that professionals take care of themselves – burnout is very real in the social media business overall, but even more so if you've been dealing with a sudden influx of angry messages.

With all that said, here's what I've landed on for best practice/toolkit for using social for crisis communications.

- Choose one or two of your most-used, most popular platforms. Keep your messaging the same on both. People need to know where to go to find information. Don't confuse them by posting different information on different platforms. I know I've been preaching about differentiating content based on platform, but this is the exception.

- Make sure that you are using social **in addition** to your owned platforms and assets, which I mentioned previously. If people are searching for information on whatever newsworthy thing is happening, you probably want your statement to come up near the top of the results, right? One way to ensure that happens is to put content on your website. Additionally, you don't have to fight algorithms on your website, and you have plenty of room to give as much context and nuance as you need.

- For social updates: for the platforms you are using for your crisis comms, make sure you know the algorithm for those platforms and work with it.

For example, as of this writing, I consider Facebook to have a "slow" algorithm, serving updates to people days after they are posted. For that reason, on Facebook, I do one post, pinned to the top, and then keep updating it with the time and date of the added information. You don't want people to keep getting served old news, especially if you decide to boost your post to get more visibility. If you have additional information on your website or other owned property, you may want to link to that from social.

- Consider the power of live updates. Southwest Airlines famously mitigated the negative sentiment from thousands of canceled flights in 2012 by using Facebook Live to keep people updated on the situation and what they were doing to solve the problem.

This tactic isn't without risk, though – you are *live*, after all. You want to have your talking points down and be prepared for whatever comments may come via your livestream.

Chapter 19

When a Special Type of S— Hits the Fan

There are a few tweaks to the last chapter's plan based on the type of crisis. These are based on my observations and experience; your mileage may vary. Of course, if the crisis situation you are dealing with is big enough – for example, your entire brand is at stake – it may be worthwhile to engage with an outside consultant.

The plan I laid out in the last chapter is best for a crisis that is largely outside your scope of control – e.g., a natural disaster. Here are a few other situations that would warrant a social media response.

Nuance 1: If the crisis is the organization or brand's fault: e.g., someone has behaved badly, or there was a major misstep.

- Put up one post with your statement, which should be cleared with legal and comms beforehand, of course.
- Strongly consider whether or not this should be a post on your timeline, where it will live forever and always be scrapable by search engines – or where it may be embarrassing for you to delete it.

CASE STUDY: The pop star versus the influencer

A few years ago, a TikTok influencer came out with an accusation that she had been pursued by and then engaged in a consensual relationship with a very married pop star. She came with receipts – she saved the DMs this star sent her from his official account (*side note*: this is what the kids call a finsta[12] is for, sir).

The star in question had pivoted from a personal brand of a bad-boy, tattooed lead singer of a band to a more family-friendly one, starring on a prime time, network TV reality show. The story wasn't a great one for him, and surely was embarrassing for his family as well. His camp was silent for a while, but once the chatter reached critical mass, they made their move – and it was masterful.

When what I can only imagine was the singer's PR firm finally released a statement, they used very careful wording: "I used poor judgment," "I crossed the line during a regrettable period in my life." But the most masterful piece of the execution wasn't in the language.

It was in the social placement.

They didn't put his statement on his Instagram or Facebook feed. Then it would live there forever, or they'd have to delete it (and

---

[12]Finsta = fake Instagram account

that would definitely get noticed and
commented upon at length).

No. They put the statement in his Instagram
stories, where things disappear after 24 hours.
So they didn't have to worry about getting rid of
the statement – and they also said, by virtue of
the placement, "This is a nothingburger."

Because if you understand the culture of
Instagram, you know that you save your grid
for your best content – the stuff you want to live
there forever. The stuff you put on your story is
the stuff you don't care about or don't want to
live on in perpetuity: the memes that resonate
in the moment; the candid photos from a party
that are funny but not necessarily flattering. By
posting the apology on his story, the pop star's
team was saying, "Read between the lines:
we're responding to this because we have to,
but this is nothing and it didn't warrant any
further attention."

And you know what? It worked. The pop
star's reputation seems to have come through
the debacle largely unscathed.

*

When a crisis is the organization or brand's doing, I find that putting your statement online can help you or hurt you. You have to tread carefully. Knowing that, here are my best practices for your social statement in this situation:

- Avoid jargon or corporate speak in your statement. Use plain language.

- If possible or appropriate, note how the mistake will be addressed.

- Move on. No further statements or comments needed.

CASE STUDY: The dating app public apology
A dating app that was famously female-friendly (founded by a woman, based on empowering its female-identifying users) rolled out a marketing campaign that did not hit the intended note. One ad in particular – which was replicated on a giant billboard in major metro areas – made light of celibacy. Which makes sense for a dating app, right? Again –

you can be so close and yet completely miss the mark.

The backlash on social media was swift and furious. The general sentiment was that the ads were "gross" and condemned the very thing the platform purported to champion – women's agency over their bodies and sexuality.

The dating app managed to pull off a masterful social media apology. In an Instagram carousel (note that they felt it was important enough to give it a place in their grid!), they gave an apology that came across as sincere and genuine. "We made a mistake." is their first line. "So, here's what we're doing," begins the section where they take accountability.

All in all, the public apology seemed to be mostly well-received and garnered even more brand mentions for the app, with articles in several online sites and news outlets, including The Verge, BBC News, and *The New York Times*.

*

Nuance 2: The crisis is the result of a company leader going rogue on a brand account.

Sometimes, despite our best efforts, people who have access to the brand accounts go rogue, and their well-intentioned – if not well-thought-out – messages can have very real consequences for the brand. That can put you in a sticky situation as an employee.

Tameka Bazile, manager of social media strategy at TIME, posted a masterful set of steps[13] to deal with this type of situation. I am paraphrasing them here but it's worth going to her LinkedIn for the full post and analysis (as well as a wealth of great advice).

- Create a brief outlining the immediate response and impact on the brand.

- Pause any scheduled content (organic and paid) that isn't connected to the current situation.

---

[13] See Tameka's full post here:
https://tinyurl.com/tamekabazile

- Work with internal teams (PR, marketing, legal) to process any discrepancies with your current brand voice.

- Outline whether an evolution of the brand voice, position and target audience is necessary, and, if not, whether a culturally relevant statement is best.

- Share findings and updates with leaders and stakeholders.

If leaders and stakeholders agree that a statement is best, I would advocate following my advice under Nuance 1.

Chapter 20

I'm Tired of Thinking of Chapter Titles, and It's Time for You to Leave the Nest and Fly, Little Baby Bird

We are wrapping up this book, and I imagine that some of you are frustrated that I have kept my advice so high-level. They want formulas. They just want someone to tell them what to post, on what platform, and how often.

I hope that you're starting to see that A) it's not that simple and b) platforms are ever evolving. I'm purposely trying to stay high-level and give caveats like "as of the time of writing," knowing that when it comes to social media, information and advice can become outdated rapidly. The basics, though – determining your strategy, evaluating and refining, rinse and repeat – don't change. They just evolve alongside the platforms.

I can't tell you what platforms to be on (unless I take the time to go through the steps we've already outlined). What I can tell you is that you don't need to be on all of them. Make sure you are on an appropriate number that meets your goals and that you/your team can keep up with. Add new platforms judiciously, because they make sense for your brand and goals – not just because it's a hot platform.

I can't give you a hashtag strategy or tell you what kind of content is going to resonate with your audience. I can – and have – given you broad recommendations, but it truly comes down to trying things, evaluating, and then trying again. Do this on a regular basis until you start seeing the results you want.

My team and I have begun meeting twice a week for thirty minutes as a strategic check-in. That may sound like a lot, but it's truly been a game changer for our efforts. In our meetings, we make sure to discuss:

Content performance: how are the things we recently put out on social performing? Anything that's really taking off, or anything that's not performing well? We discuss why there are outliers in either direction.

Sentiment trends: if we start seeing a general trend in the comments or incoming messages, we make sure to discuss it as a group. It may be something we need to address with our content, or something we should alert company leaders to.

Online trends: we talk about the things that we've seen on our social media feeds that have caught our attention. To combat the bias of our own algorithms, we also look at trending topics on Google Trends and use their Explore tool, narrowed down to the Health category (since we work for a health system), to see what people are searching for. It's also useful for us to look at what autofills in YouTube's search bar and what comes up in the research tab of YouTube analytics to help us see what kind of content our audiences are currently consuming.

Remember that in this game, flexibility is crucial. You always have to be prepared to pivot: on your strategy, on your content plans, even on the way you do social media. The platforms will change – not to mention their algorithms. Crises will happen. Content you felt sure would be a hit will flop, and content you expected to bomb will unexpectedly take off.

Working on social media is like holding a handful of sand – squeeze it too tight, and it will start getting away from you.

Keep it loose, and you'll be much happier – and more successful in your efforts.

*

In the end, social media marketing is difficult because people think of it with the emphasis on *marketing* rather than on *social media*.

In other words, they think of it as just another platform to use as a megaphone for their brand messaging.

But it's not. It's a conversation. It's back and forth. And if you enter a conversation with a megaphone, if you treat it as a one-way channel to blast whatever message you feel like amplifying, people will generally leave.

Imagine you're on a city street in a casual, hip shopping district. It's a hot day, but despite the oppressive heat, there's some guy wearing a button-down shirt, buttoned ALL the way up, dark pants, and dress shoes. His hair is slicked severely to the side and he has a microphone plugged into a small portable speaker. As you approach, you can make out what he is yelling into the microphone. "The earth is flat!" he shouts. "Don't continue down this street or you will fall off! Buy my protection spray for just $5!"

Whether it's out of amusement, curiosity or general concern, you stop to try to reason with the guy. The earth is not flat, and the street certainly does not end in a precipitous cliff drop into space, you try to tell him. You've walked down it thousands of times. You come here often. You know this neighborhood. And besides, you've taken basic science classes. On the other hand, you've never seen this guy, and the way he's presenting himself – completely at odds with his surroundings – doesn't really lend him much credibility.

But when you try to talk to the guy, he doesn't seem to want to engage, especially when he sees that you don't have your wallet out. Instead, he turns his back to you and shouts louder into his microphone.

In case the metaphor is not completely clear: too often, social media marketing acts like the guy with the microphone.

When you look at it that way, it's not hard to understand why a lot of efforts fall flat, right? Your audience wants to feel like they're being listened to. You're in *their* neighborhood, and they want to feel like they have a voice, like you get them, like you want something more than just to sell them something.

One way to give your audience a voice is to build your online community, and that's certainly important. But I hope what you've taken away from this book is that you must listen to the feedback your audience is giving you by *paying attention*. What are they posting on the platforms you want to be on? How are they reacting to what you are posting? Are you adding value to their feeds or adding noise? If you start with a strategic framework, you'll be able to evaluate your efforts more effectively.

Be the brand that adds value. The one that educates, entertains, or informs (or better yet, all three!). Build trust. Build brand awareness. Build a relationship with your audience. And then the sales – or clicks, or engagement, or whatever your goal is! – will come. And beyond that, you're going to have more fun with it. Be careful – working on your social media marketing might just become your favorite part of your day.

Acknowledgments

So many people helped me with the creation of this book, and I owe a debt of gratitude to them all. Thank you to Elizabeth Jacobs, proofreader extraordinaire, who was able to work on the tightest deadline ever. Katie Sterner, the designer for the cover of this book, is not only a talented artist but a true friend. Thank you to Erin Johanning, who took a chance on a marketing copywriter and put her in charge of a company Facebook page, kicking off a fun and fruitful stage of my career. Thank you to Riley Munin for guiding me through the publishing process with humor and patience. Finally, last but not least, thank you to my editor and mentor, Robert J. Sawyer, for coaching me, building me up again and again, and believing in me. You're truly the reason I am writing.

And to all the people who heard the concept of this book and said "YES, that is what we need, please keep going," thank you. I hope I've given you something that helps you as much as you've helped me.

About the Author

Amanda F. Potter is an award-winning content strategist and social media manager based out of Sioux Falls, South Dakota. She currently oversees content strategy for the nation's largest rural healthcare system, where she and her team oversee over 75 social media accounts. Amanda is a prolific writer, an engaging public speaker and trainer, and a fair-weather outdoorswoman. Find her online and subscribe to her monthly newsletter about social media, content creation, personal branding and online culture at AmandaFPotter.com

www.ingramcontent.com/pod-product-compliance
Lightning Source LLC
Chambersburg PA
CBHW071422210326

41597CB00020B/3621

9781962699273